IT MANAGERS - A Mutation of the **Human Species,** or Just a **Mindset** Issue

IT MANAGERS - A Mutation of the **Human Species,** or Just a **Mindset** Issue

KUNAL THAKUR

PARTRIDGE

A Penguin Random House Company

To order additional copies of this book, contact
Partridge India
000 800 10062 62
www.partridgepublishing.com/india
orders.india@partridgepublishing.com

CONTENTS

Dedication

To my parents who taught me to know the difference between right and wrong, to be empathetic, and most of all, try to be a good human being and a man of values. To all my friends (they know whom all I mean) who have tolerated me, advised me, corrected me, and always shown faith in me. Without any of these people, I wouldn't have been able to take this book up. And not the least, all my colleagues who have sometimes reported to me, who inspired me more than anyone else to try to be a good manager.

Acknowledgement

I express my gratitude to some of the people because of whom this book became a reality. To my close ones, who supported me for taking up this endeavour. To my friends, who read the book over and over again to point out mistakes, suggested improvements to the book, shared with me their personal experiences and anecdotes.

I thank my publishers because of whom I was able to publish the book in its present form. I also thank the editors who proofread the book and rectified the mistakes I had made.

Special mention to my parents who have never stopped me from taking on any endeavour. My extra special friends, who have more faith in me than I have in myself. To my seniors, in the organisations where I worked in the past, who always guided me. Many of the thoughts and lessons are inspired from their guidance. Special mention for Dheeraj for the cover design.

Last but not the least, to the software techie (which even I was one at some point) whose struggles and perspectives led to the idea of this book.

THE BEGINNING

First of all, I would like to say that this book is not intended to hurt the sentiments, beliefs, and ideas of anyone. The idea of the book came to me one day while I was in conversation with one of my colleagues. That's when a thought struck me that I had conversations on these issues with numerous professionals umpteen number of times, and there was so much that was needed to be said out loud. Resultantly, I thought, it would be better to put the random incidents, ideas, and observations, taking 'rounds' in my head, in an organised form. I had several occasions to observe the perspectives of the subordinates on a project team in an IT company. Almost every day, we as team members exchanged volley of views on our management as to how it is versus how it should be. After I became a manager, I always tried to bear in mind what I felt and experienced when I was a part of the development team. I based my behaviour and actions on them. I attempted to become a manager that was congruent to a notion as to what kind of manager I would have loved to work for. It encouraged me and provided me with an impetus to be able to create the best possible environment for the team. I realised, however, that it was not as easy a task as I had apprehended in my head. A simple idea for a change turned into a mammoth task as I was not the only one responsible in bringing about these changes. There were people above me too. What was bothersome was that some of them still had that 'traditional' way of 'managing' things and people. Couple of times, I was even asked why I was very friendly with the team. This attitude and approach was highly annoying and repulsive to me. Experiences like these made me realise how things come from someone up and boil down to the team members below, which then ultimately result in a really difficult attitude and atmosphere in the team— an attitude that the team not only needs to be highly productive but sometimes unrealistically productive. I do not intend to target managers as a whole. After all, I have seen and worked with some great managers. It was because of them that I myself learnt a lot. But, in general, majority of them need to bring about a genuine shift in their attitude and perspective. My book is an attempt to surface those managers who still practice the old way, which doesn't go down well with a qualified team. It is also for those subordinates who think managers do not have any work, and trust me, there are a lot of subordinates who think that. It primarily is an attempt to bring out the subordinate's perspective; however, in some cases, it also brings out the manager's perspective which subordinates need to understand in order to introduce a wholesome healthy work environment. I hope people find something relevant and useful in this book and be able to just practice 'management' in a more humane way.

Why this was the right time for me to pen down this work? Because, now being a manager myself, I could compare and construe a hopefully meaningful analogy of the both sides and my thoughts would definitely hold more value than they would have held had I not experienced life on both ends. I am not prejudiced against the managers here. I am myself one. And that is why I, more than anyone else, want that managers are thought of as someone good, rather people cringing at my name or designation. That is what I think and hope all managers would love to see.

IT'S MY TURN NOW TO PLAY THE MUSIC!

Created using www.dinospike.com

He walks in the office and suddenly seems to be a different person than he was yesterday. The air of authority has seeped in him through the night. The once relatively friendly person has become colder. He has suddenly acquired a profound understanding of the organisational processes and objectives along with forgetting about how it is to be normal. He does the same things which he objected, criticised, and sometimes rebelled against till yesterday. What changed? The day before he was promoted to the project manager for a software team. *Dude, what got into this thickhead so fast? Why can't anyone deal with being a manager properly?* remarked one teammate to other.

The anecdote rings a bell. Doesn't it? This is what many software engineers across India would relate to. The one who steps up the ladder seems to forget what he cribbed about, almost instantly, when the designation change happens. Or at least, the so-called subordinates definitely feel that way. Result, manager becomes something as abhorrent as anything else they can think of.

Teammate 1: Hey, I have seen, I am more productive and happy to work when the manager is on leave. What you think?

Teammate 2: Seriously, I do not know why they are even there? What do they do except people-bashing and trying to suck out every small or big mistake and throw it at you during appraisals, to save some peanuts for the company. Seems like slavery would have been a more exciting time than these.

These conversations are very common in the IT Industry. The root cause is that the managers still have the traditional mindset about getting the work done by the employees by just using authority and power in an anarchic way—the very same qualities which they resented when they were down the ladder. Slowly and gradually, the person playing the role of manager has become one of the most hated positions by the subordinates in the Indian IT industry. Traditional way of just pushing and instructing people, with an air of authority, doesn't go down well with the employees who feel that things could be done much better in a different way. In my career earlier, as a software developer, I came across managers who worked more like policeman rather than leading a team of qualified knowledge workers. Snooping around to see what the employee is browsing on the net or what playlists he is making to listen to songs while working gives a perception to the employees that managers are more concerned with these activities rather than the deliverable work they output.

One of my colleagues once said to me, *My manager never sees when I put in extra time or weekends to get a deliverable in, but always sees and tracks that I spent half an hour away from the seat when I went for a coffee or smoke break. Why the hell doesn't he join the vigilance or security forces, because he is bloody good at it?*

Courtesy: stripgenerator.com

Scolding, reprimanding, or more commonly used term by employees known as bashing is not the only way to get some work done by someone else. I agree it is sometimes required and imperative to use this method. But managers have a bigger role than this, and they actually do a lot of work than what people see. Why not appear a little human to your subordinates rather than a mechanical machine which only triggers when some work has to be got done or when a piece of your mind has to be given to the subordinates?

Power tactics do not work well anymore. One of my senior HR managers once wisely said, 'People do not leave companies as much as they leave their managers.' Traditional management styles were apt and effective in different times. Thinking should not be like 'I faced it as a subordinate so it's my turn now to use the same powers and make people work, by making it fearful and difficult for them.' The thought that prevails predominantly is that managers are just fault-finding machines and never trust and believe that people actually want to work and will do the job. Rather, it should be the other way round that people inherently want to work and you trust them to do it and manage their time themselves, as long as the overall goal of the project or phase is not compromised. And I have seen it myself, after I became a manager, that more you trust people, the better they work and more respect you earn. After all, I am sure the only motive in the life of a manager is not just to fulfil the Key Performance Indicators (KPIs) but also to be respected and looked up to by his peers and more importantly, his juniors. It is then that even the subordinates will see a manager as a part of the human species too. If managers think for their subordinates, I can assure that the team will stand up for and with him in any difficulty. No manager then would even have to ask a team member to put in extra effort to get some deliverable in. Your team will do it because they respect you and see that even you are vulnerable, you also face lot of pressure, and given a choice, you wouldn't exploit them or make them slog. They won't like it themselves if they let you down.

Chuck the traditional way. Be human, be more connected to individuals, individually rather than just collectively as a team.

In one of my projects, I was facing flak from senior management about the progress of the project. I knew the team was putting in the efforts despite various limitations in skills and experience, and I stood with them. I connected with each one of them individually, and people who on record had never ever came on weekends to put in work hours, themselves, said to me that they will do it without me asking them. My boss had instructed me to tell the team to work on weekends, but I never even had to. Team also realised that even I was under pressure and trying my best not to transfer a whole of it onto them, especially, in an unpleasant way or in a way that said, 'I had the power to do so, and they had to oblige.' When you know you have authority, scolding or ordering someone is the easiest of things to do. Initially, many times, I felt that why should I be listening for some slip ups by the team. Then, I remembered a conversation with one of my seniors in my first job. I just remarked lightly to him that manager was such a great role as you had the authority to drive things as per you and boss people around. To this, he replied that being a manager is not easy. People will always say that managers do nothing, and most of all, a manager's role entails being a shock absorber for the team so that the team can perform at the highest quality.

It's only when I became one that I realised that one had to be a shock absorber better than those installed in a Hummer, which is mighty tough to match. Both the sides have to trust. After all no one likes being chided for someone else's doings, and a manager is bound to snap. A manager is in the firing line from both sides of the ladder and that explains the behaviour sometimes exhibited by us. I remembered the insight from my senior that helped me be more rational and empathetic to some extent. It is tough, but the new generation manager has to think on these lines.

Manager: This is not acceptable and cannot be tolerated. I don't care what happened or not but this has to be fixed anyhow and I don't care how you do it.

Subordinate: But . . .

Manager: I don't want excuses. Just ensure this should not happen again.

(Manager leaves)

Subordinate (to a teammate): What is wrong with this bugger? Doesn't let you speak and explain, and even when he does, doesn't understand it or maybe lets it out the other ear. I stayed here till late night working on this. If I didn't want to do it, why would I have stayed? Why the managers always are scared of clients even on things for which sometimes nothing more could be done? Why are they there if they can't listen or explain these things to the client? If he is so perfect, one of these days, I will put up my hand and tell him to do it himself and then see what he does. At max what will he do? May be impact my hike or get me fired. Well, there is no shortage of jobs for my role and experience. Worst part is the way he talks, as if I am a primary school kid doing something naughty in class, and he preaches to everyone the importance of communication, when he himself can't practice any of it.

Traditionally, it was the manager who was the knowledge centre in an organisation. But in IT, it's not the same in today's scenario. The knowledge centre is the team a manager manages. In such a case, it is absurd to think that an anarchic attitude will go down well with people who are the ones, actually doing the work. The communication style and management approach have to change. If disliked, it is because of their own actions. There is a need for managers to understand that they are not supermen and neither are they expected to be. But if only they accept this and their fallibility as well and treat people with respect, none of these perceptions will build. Reprimanding is sometimes imperative for repeated mistakes and carelessness, but it has to be properly packaged so as not to attack or hurt the self-esteem of the person but to attack the repeating issue and its bigger impact to business or client. One of my seniors said to me early in my career, 'Give some slack to the people sometimes, and it is surprising how they respond once they understand the impact that some of their actions had and how much the manager had to deal with it on their behalf, standing up for them.' I have seen and experienced this, and it works wonders.

<u>Moral:</u> Being a manager is not like ragging in college (not that I support ragging) that since you got ragged in first year and absolutely hated it, you have the right and liberty to rag your juniors to take it out when they come in. With time, even traditions and cultures change. It's time management approach with regards to people also changed.

IF YOU FORGET WHAT
YOU WERE, YOU WILL
NEVER KNOW WHAT
YOU WILL BECOME

Teammate 1: Why doesn't our manager live and let live? He is always frowning. I think he should get married now. It's high time. Plus he would take a few days off and it might lighten him up too.

Teammate 2: I so wish he goes on a really long honeymoon, misses his flight while coming back, and is further delayed by at least a week.

Teammate 1: Leave it. You know you are not that lucky for these wishes to come true.

Teammate 2: Dude, I am not even asking just for me. I am doing some good to him too. Imagine that long honeymoon changes him, and he returns a changed angelic man! Okay now, I agree that this is too much of wishful thinking, but I think he needs a break, or he will end up driving all of us to suicide.

After few years, the Teammate 1 eventually became a manager himself.

Created using stripgenerator.com

Senior Manager: !@#$$%%^&&*
Manager (Teammate 1): Sure, I will take care of it.

Later,

Manager to a subordinate: !@#$$%%^&&*!@#$$% %^&&*!@#$$%%^&&*

This is a chain reaction, and it is this thing we as managers need to stop. And this is precisely why after a certain time, even small mistakes by the team result in bloodbath. Manager is not the king in the company, and subordinates should know that and realise that he is also under pressure. So if the team makes him look bad in front of his boss, the manager snaps and takes it out.

When I became a manager, even my first instinct was to give the team a good hiding. I thought, 'I never even listened to my parents when I knew it was not my fault, and because of the team, I am listening from my manager.' But then I remembered something my father said to me once. He said, *'Never forget your roots and what you faced coming up to the point where you are. But since you are there now, it is your responsibility to correct the things you didn't like earlier. But remember it won't be easy.'*

I realised 'won't be easy' was the mildest of terms to use for that situation. It took efforts, but at least to some extent I was able to do it, and surprisingly, the team saw that, understood, and realised I was taking those efforts only for them. I was only letting them know what had to be improved without all the unpleasant stuff. Result, they visibly became more responsible and careful.

There is one more thing. My dad hardly used to even scold me for anything. The scolding and hiding was my mom's department. So by the time I reached college, it was like a day wasn't complete if Mom didn't scold me. On the other hand, I am still wary of my dad being angry and scolding me. The important point is anger is a good weapon and so it should be used judiciously; otherwise, after a while, it becomes just another thing without any impact.

As we keep growing up starting as a kid, our sense of self-evaluation becomes highly biased towards ourselves. We rebel against almost everything. We hardly listen to what parents say and try to teach us. Then there comes a time when we suddenly realise that we are not 'know-all'. It is then we know what we were taught as kids was meant for now when we had enough sense. If at this juncture we can remember those things, I think all of us managers would be much better at dealing with people and understanding them.

When I joined my second company after engineering, one of my friends was struggling a little bit on the health front for which he had to take frequent sick leaves. He was called by the manager, and this is what followed.

Manager: Again you took a day off. It cannot work like this. We have lots to complete.

My friend: I understand, but I cannot help it if I am not well.

Manager: I don't know whether that is even the case or it is just made-up excuse.

This really offended him, as he was really ill and unable to come. I knew people indulged in fake reasons to take off days for a day or two, but that doesn't give anybody a reason to doubt someone else like in this particular case. He was so upset with the remark that he later told me that he talked back.

My friend: Well, I understand that you might have come across such situations but that doesn't give you a right to question or belittle my problem. If you are so wary, please hire some private detectives for each employee to verify their sick leaves, but you cannot question me until you actually bump into me somewhere outside when I have taken a leave on grounds of sickness. If that happens, you may do whatever you want.

He came out and told me that if his manager wanted to fire him for this, so be it. It anyways is not worth slogging for a company like that. That issue was finally settled without further aggravation, but incidents like these really tick the employees off.

Created using stripgenerator.com

When I became a manager and one of the team members was taking little frequent unplanned leaves, I doubted him too. I had no concrete proof against him, so I could not say anything to him, and I remembered the situation with my friend years ago. Maybe he had a genuine problem too and that is the benefit of doubt that had to be given.

On the other hand, if the rapport between team members and the manager is great, the manager will automatically come to know the reasons for leaves because team members will be very truthful. I have been extremely truthful with managers with whom a rapport was built, and with the managers who were always distant, I will admit I lied too. It is human behaviour.

Created using dinospike.com

For the above kind of conversations to happen, the employees have to be candid, and candour has to flow freely throughout the organisation. Each manager asks and expects the team members to be candid.

Teammate: What is this all about candour and truthfulness these guys keep talking about? Will he grant me leave if I tell him I feel like resting today because of overwork past week and there is not much work right now? He will give me all sorts of 'gyan' and professionalism and how things work. It's better I lie rather than listen and feel as if I am attending those Osho or Ramdev Baba sermons.

Subordinates expect reciprocity whenever possible, and it's only then the candour can become part of the culture. On the other hand, managers cannot entertain every kind of request every time, and it is when the manager should take effort to explain to the subordinate their personal and professional limitations and predicament as well. Just brushing people off doesn't work well.

I once approached my manager regarding little change of my leave days. I wanted the whole set of five-day leaves shifted by one day. I thought there was nothing 'rocket science' in it as I was not increasing my leaves. But my manager expressed concern, and my first reaction in my head was *What the hell, how does shifting one day create an issue?* He then explained to me the situation as it was and how tough it was. Other team members were also on leave, and the project could not afford zero work on even one day as it was in critical phase. He asked for a day's time and told that he will try to work things around but could not commit that my leaves would be approved. I understood. Next day, in the evening, he came and informed me that my leave dates were shifted by one day as I have asked and that everything is all right for me to avail the leave. He himself also seemed happy that I could go on my leave as I wanted. From that day on, I knew that he wouldn't ruin or put boulders in my way when it came to leaves and I felt comfortable telling about day offs even if the reason may seem petty for others but important to me. It felt good to know that managers are not there just to screw you up but are bound sometimes, and I always had in mind that he must have put his neck out to let me go; hence, I ensured that I don't let him down.

Well, I chose leaves to elucidate the problem because it is one of the most common grounds of dissent. It is not that I am just obsessed with leaves or that is the only issue that prevails. It is in many cases similar to this where trust becomes non-existent.

<u>Moral:</u> Do not forget what you went through and felt when you were down the ladder. After that you won't have to worry about where you are going. Your feet and head would be in the right direction always.

IT'S NOT 1820
OR EVEN 1990,
FOR THAT MATTER

Created using stripgenerator.com and dinospike.com

Teammate 1: Americans will say that slavery ended in 1860. I want them to come and have a look here.

Teammate 2: True. In any other field, an engineer is treated like, okay, great, he is an engineer! In IT, we engineers are treated sometimes like labourers.

I myself had a similar conversation with one of my friends who was an engineer in Bajaj Motors, and he told me that people treated engineers with reverence. They were the ones who did and got work done. They were the knowledge hub. But in IT, in majority of cases, I have observed that there is serious lack of respect. Sometimes it's because of some of the managers who think they are 'know-all' or think they are the ones actually running the show. However, nothing is farther from the truth. The IT tech team is the knowledge sink of an IT company. True, management is the one who brings in work, but the actual core work is carried out by these professionals. It is natural for these professionals to feel that way. They too slogged hours in studying engineering and spent money to get that education, but many times, they are not treated like qualified people. I myself felt when I was working as a developer that being bossed around too much was not cool. I thought so many times *I am a bloody engineer and a good one at that, why this treatment as if I don't know anything and am at the mercy of the manager?*

The main problem is not with being bossed around. Subordinates should and will understand that there is a lot more at stake for the manager and he has to get the work done. Manager is the boss and has the authority to behave like one sometimes. He cannot always be a friend. The problem is sometimes it is the way that bossing around is done that ticks the self-esteem of people. What managers need to understand is that these are the qualified white-collared professionals who have aspirations, prestige, pride, and motivation to be in that job. They cannot be talked to in a way which hurts any of these in any way. It is not like managing a team of labourers where the sole aim for workers is to get enough to get by for that day. Line managers in manufacturing setups resort to shouting, scolding, micromanaging and so on to get the work done from them. That is not how management will work in IT though.

My senior once told me, *Give people under you respect even when they do not expect it, and they will work for you like anything just for that.* I realised how true it was when I became a manager. If managers show their vulnerability just a little bit and accept that no matter how much the authority, it is the people he commands that are going to do the job and treat them so there won't be much issues.

A senior consultant in my team in my first job was one such person. He was ever so respectful even while pointing out mistakes that we juniors always made sure not to let him down at any cost. We voluntarily cancelled our leaves couple of times because we felt he might have to bear it or overwork if we left at that critical time. That was a perfect two-way harmony. I was myself surprised. Unless I am on the cricket field or on a bike trip, I love to lazy around. I can just keep lying down and stare at the walls for hours and be that lazy. Imagine my reluctance to go and work on a weekend. But when it came to some work for the senior consultant, I never felt even a hint of reluctance to go and put in work even on a weekend. Managers need to take a leaf out of that book. Managers today are more of facilitators and analysts as to why some problem is happening and how to help the team work around it. They cannot afford to show that they are the boss (even if they are). Managers need to show that people work with him and not for him.

On the other hand, subordinates should not be complaining if they get something from manager for some repetitive misses and carelessness. They understand it or not, but there is lot on manager's plate all the time. And believe it or not, managers have a whole lot more at stake than the tech guys, and they cannot afford to patiently tolerate too many lapses from the team. It is like those elder siblings in the house getting scolded for the doings of their younger ones. It was damn annoying for me. But imagine the same at the corporate professional level. It is not a pleasant situation to be in, and subordinates need to understand that perspective. Therefore, it again has to be two-way. May be managers have to take initiative and show it first to build trust. The team will then reciprocate.

Teammate 1: Why doesn't our manager trust anyone? Other day, I caught him snooping behind me as to what I was doing. I was making a playlist. When I saw him, he told me to work, other things will keep happening. I replied to him that it is because of these other things that work is happening, otherwise I am not a machine that can be programmed to work for set number of hours without doing anything else.

Teammate 2: Man, he must have been pissed off at you then. Let it be, why get into mud and let managers form a bad perception of us? Be careful.

Teammate 1: I don't care, dude. I mean I work better with listening to music. What he has got to do with it? I am giving him work. He should be happy with that. If something is wrong with my work, then he has all the rights to pull me up. I chose this field and this job. I want to do it and excel at it. Then why he treats everyone as if all of us just want to shirk work all the time. It is offending and insulting at times.

Created using dinospike.com

Teammate 1: I think we have a job more like security guards. Come to office on time and then stay till crazy hours. Even security guards rotate, but we don't.

Teammate 2: Ha ha! What else you thought you would get after getting into this industry? Especially for people like us who are new in it out of college. In a metro, you cannot find any person to work for you in Rs. 12,000 per month except a software engineer. Even the spot boys in films get Rs. 800 a day, and 'auto drivers' make around 25,000 per month. And they say we are the white-collar guys. It's hilarious, especially when we actually do work which is intellectual and 'cutting edge' in most cases. On top of that, we get all sorts of policing. I think they forget after hiring that they hire engineers.

Keeping the financial part aside, the factors are easier to control for the managers and the organisation. Just giving everyone the due respect, acknowledging their work, trusting them, and talking to them not like a boss but just like a senior colleague will put majority of them at ease. It is when even managers will see heightened motivation and responsibility levels from the employees. It is not that tough if thought about with a clear mind.

<u>Moral:</u> People working in IT are qualified professionals with good educational background. So they expect to be treated a certain way even when the situations are tough with the boss. Tough and hard talks should be direct and frank but not rude and hurting. After all, there is a very fine line in being frank and outright rude.

ONE SIZE
DOESN'T FIT ALL!

Created using dinospike.com

Teammate 1: You know what, I have to work this weekend. Manager just told me. And you won't believe, I 'might get a comp-off and free lunch.' As if that's all I am living for.

Teammate 2: Dude, that's amazing. You have an amazing life. (Laughs out loud!)

Teammate 1: I don't understand. For the management, the only way to incentivise or motivate is free lunch and comp-off. And what's more interesting is that the same methods are used for everyone.

Teammate 2: It's not an ideal world, my friend.

Teammate 1: No, seriously, I don't want lunch and comp-off. I have indicated many times that I would love to work myself if given something new, more challenging, or cutting edge. I would myself come and work without free lunch and comp-off. How difficult it is to figure out that not everyone needs the same things to excite them. It is like giving someone a "Mango bite" candy when one wants to Learn to make a pastry cake.

Teammate 2: What to say? For me, all I sometimes need is just a little bit of appreciation and acknowledgement that I am doing some important and good work. His appreciations even if they come out, come only at predefined times like quarterly awards time. He thinks people don't need anything in between those three months. Self-motivation is fine, and I do that, but sometimes after a gruelling day if your boss just even says informally that you did a good job, it gives you something to work the next day.

The point to be noted is that motivation is one thing which cannot be administered in a group all the time. A manager is supposed to be the leader of the team, and a leader knows his team members closely. Knowing is the key word here. Not just by name and what they work on, but personally, individually, and empathetically knows every one of them. He needs to know what makes each of his team members tick. Every individual is different with a distinct personality. Therefore, each is motivated by something different from the other. Consider this, what if the Indian cricket team captain Dhoni tried to motivate the cricketer Suresh Raina by telling he would get extra match fees if he did some fast bowling. Will that be motivation? He would have to tell Raina that the team would need him in a critical situation and the team is relying on him to finish the match with the bat. You can see what would work and what would not. I used this example because we know these people relatively more than we know about our co-workers with whom we work every day.

Teammate 1: This weekend, I experienced a funny thing while out shopping in the local market.

Teammate 2: Tell me.

Teammate 1: I was looking to buy a shirt and finally selected one. The shopkeeper, though, was asking too much for it, considering that it was not branded stuff. I haggled a bit with him for a price which I thought was fair. He said that if I wanted discount, I could buy the other shirt. The shirt was like a flashy third-grade kind of thing. I told him, dude, I don't want the discount. I want this particular shirt at a fair price. It is like I have come to buy a shirt and you are offering me underwear saying that underwear is cheaper, buy it. You should have seen the look in his face. But then, suddenly, I remembered our manager. He has a similar concept of incentives I think. People here need shirts, as to say, and he offers underwear. It's amazing understanding.

The key to motivation is involvement. The key is connecting with everyone at their level. You cannot connect with a fresh graduate using the same way as you would try to connect with an experienced member. It is imperative to be observant. In all the madness of monitoring process compliances and tracking progresses, managers miss out on this aspect. That is why leaders are different from managers. Motivation is totally a people's art, if we talk in people management terms. And that is being a leader. That is why people always swear by leaders and loathe managers. Having being a manager myself, I would not like being the latter. Managers, thus, need to strive to be the former, and they will themselves be surprised to see how readily and eagerly their team would work with them.

When I started my career, one of my seniors, who eventually came to know me little more personally than others, observed that I liked to work on new things. Working on same things over an extended period bored me. So, whenever something new used to come up, he started pulling me also in it and that rejuvenated my enthusiasm to work. Result was that no matter how much effort it took, I was ever so eager and ready to work with him and for him.

Anybody can be a leader, and a leader doesn't need a designation. However, the converse is not true. A manager ought to be a leader more so because he has that designation. He can make a much bigger impact. In a way, he has the power to make and break people. So it is imperative that he closely knows his team members. If a team member is not getting motivated enough, then maybe he is not being motivated the right way. Managers think they did enough to motivate but still didn't see any, which then results in poor perception and feedback for that member. Manager is right in his own way. He cannot keep trying and investing in one person repeatedly, but it is not the person's fault either. He was simply not nudged in a right way. Managers need to understand and motivate each team member appropriately so that each one of them is ticked individually.

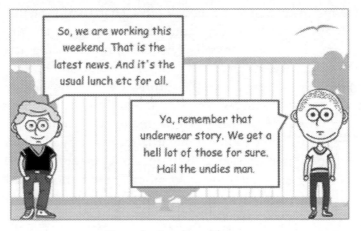

Created using dinospike.com

People do not always need much to get motivated or feel good about themselves. Sometimes, it is just an acknowledgement that a person is vital to the team. For some, it is frequent appreciations, however small it may be. One thing is for sure, you will never find someone complain about extra appreciation. But they will always complain about lack of it. For some, it is just more and more challenging work. For some, it is as simple as doing a well-defined work so that they predict and balance their work and life. Hence, it is different for each one and that is the job of manager to find out and validate. By just coming to a conclusion on an observation might not be fully correct either.

This is more important for the young generation managers who are getting into the industry to be aware of these things. Older people would not be able to change much, for they have been practicing few things for ages now and it is not easy to change. If we want the industry and the way it operates with regards to people to change, the young will have to start the change.

<u>Moral:</u> Motivation is like food. Every individual has his/her own taste and different amount of spices that they would like in the dish. So spice it up according to the person concerned.

IT'S NOT A PRIMARY SCHOOL

Teammate 1: When is your 'feedback session'?

Teammate 2: No. It is hardly that. It is 'you did this wrong, you did that wrong' session.

Teammate 1: Hope you get through this. See on the other side.

Teammate 2: Oh, I will. After first two lines of badgering, do you think I even hear the rest? He has to blabber because it is in the process, and I just have to lend an ear for few minutes. That is all it is.

Feedback sessions across companies, knowingly or unknowingly, focus increasingly more on finding and pointing out the mistakes done by the employees. Even the meaning of the word is not even close to that. Feedback is a communication loop. Managers have to listen and not just pretend to listen and then carry on with their agenda. Feedback has to be about both positive and negative. The negative feedback has to be packaged in such a way that people are receptive to it when it is put out to them. In my personal experience, whenever the feedback session has become purely fault-pointing or badgering session, I have automatically shut down after first few lines and just waited for it to be over. And that is exactly not the purpose of those sessions. The purpose is to let the people know what they have done great, what they have done well, and where they fell short. After that they need to be presented with suggestions as to how to overcome the shortcomings. The suggestions can't be in a reprimanding form because they might work only sometimes on some people at best. It has to be in a way that you are solving a problem which is not just the employee's concern but a bigger problem which both the parties have to find a solution to.

In most of the organisations, I came to know from friends, the only feedback session they have is the year-end appraisal. That is a very long horizon to keep track of. An employee who worked very well throughout the year but if towards the end something didn't go that well, the manager will remember the lapse and that would affect the appraisal. Sometimes, managers tend to lose focus and base their feedback on the recent happenings rather than the effort of whole year. When this happens, the employees are bound to feel that management just has to come up with excuses for not giving a good appraisal even though that might not be true. In my personal experience, once I was talking to one of my team members who had done some great work. In this organisation, there were two official reviews in a year. But even then the observation was that what you do in the second half is what counts and the first one somehow gets lost. So, no matter how many reviews are there, it doesn't matter unless they are used properly. One of my friend's manager used to keep a personal note of each of his team members throughout the year like a running document. And he used to refer to each of the points he had noted in course of the year and discuss in the year-end review. Surprisingly, none of my friend's colleagues and my friend ever had a complaint against him as to how the discussion went. This aspect is also very important when we want these sessions to be actually effective.

Well, I am not an expert on the subject or a psychologist, but by simple common sense, I myself experienced when I actually listened to the manager and when not. When I became manager, I tried to do it the way I thought was better. It worked much better so much so that afterwards, some of those people themselves came up to me and said that they were implementing the suggestions and advice and themselves felt they were doing better. I am not saying I am the only one right. But if someone as new as me in management could think a little and try a different approach, I am sure others can too. They just need a will. I am also sure if senior people put a mind to it, because of their vast experience, they would come with amazing ways to actually make this feedback session constructive. At the moment, in majority of the cases, I see managers just rendering lip service about making it constructive, but when the moment comes, no one cares and remembers. The subordinates are bound to block out that process if they feel like that.

Teammate 1 (with a wink): How was your 'feedback session'? You look in 'great' spirits.

Teammate 2: It was amazing. This time I set a personal record. I blocked out after the opening line itself. What's more, I thought all about how I am going to spend the coming weekend in that half an hour inside my head, while the guy was blabbering along to glory. I don't even feel like justifying anything because he is not interested in it.

Teammate 1: That is not fair. The guy in the cabin thinks he did a hell of a job. You just wasted his efforts.

Teammate 2: To hell with his efforts. Only things he says is that this is not acceptable, that is not acceptable, you did this wrong, you did that wrong, and this should not happen again, blah, blah, blah. As if, I am here earning a salary for just doing mistakes and listening to him. And going by other people's experiences, no one has ever done anything worthwhile here. Why the hell then are all these people including me are here? Why doesn't he do everything himself? Mr Perfect.

Teammate 1: His sole job is to follow the process. He does that. That's it. He doesn't care what utility is there. Or, maybe it's too much effort or beyond him to make it constructive.

Teammate 2: Whatever, I am done for now and will take a break.

Created using dinospike.com

I think, as long as we keep the listeners receptive to feedback and drive the point home rather than attack the person, it should be fine. I agree, maybe not always, but it should do on most occasions and could me more productive. Few points which I have observed by in generally observing people from both sides of the table are as follows:

People want to hear about the good they have done too. Anyone cannot have done everything bad. There is some good even in disasters. When people listen to that, they believe manager is fair and would listen to the negative as well. Otherwise, it just makes them defensive straightaway, and no matter how wrong they might have done, they won't accept it internally and so the problem remains.

There is a limit to how much people can listen to negative things about them. It needs to be sprinkled with positives however small they may be for people to listen and agree to negatives.

There is never a need to attack the person. Attacking the issue is important. Negatives are improvement areas; some need less improvement some more. But as long as they are addressed as improvement areas and not pure shortcomings of the person, people are receptive and work towards correcting them.

Created using dinospike.com

Scolding method doesn't work. Even to a kid, too much scolding turns him into a rebel. We are talking about adult, experienced, and qualified professionals.

People are not resources. They are beings. They have a brain and a heart. Nothing can come out nudging either one too much.

No one, no manager has the right to be rude with a feedback. Statements like 'What the hell you did?' or 'What is this bullshit?' or even remotely similar language would ever do any good. What's worse, if the employee escalates it, manager might get into trouble. So it's not good for anyone.

Be objective about just the problem. Don't become personal.

Use examples of mistakes and suggest examples of ways of doing the thing the correct way.

It is important to tell the person that what improvements have been seen from the last time.

Make the person believe that you are with them and not against them and want them to do well and improve.

Be empathetic. Sometimes the reason for a mistake might be a totally unrelated occurrence. People have personal lives too.

Don't try to sound as know-all. Suggest improvements and ask the person about how the issue could be solved according to him.

Discuss. Don't give judgements.

Don't show (by words or body language) or behave as if you have the power and authority. The person knows it already. Instead, be humble and connect with them at their level, and they will be receptive.

These things have worked well for me in my short career, and I have noted them down over a period of time. I am sure the amount of experience there is in management level in Indian IT industry, if given a thought they would come up with something really amazing.

From a manager's perspective, I would want the person I am giving feedback to, to be very receptive, participating, and able to accept and work towards improvements. But for that to happen, managers have to take the first step forward that the person trusts him and sees the value in that discussion.

<u>Moral:</u> Even as a child, too much scolding or hearing too much negative things about ourselves made us rebels or short of confidence. Adults are equally prone too and that is not what we want in a knowledge-based industry. So young managers, chuck the boss attitude and pick up the problem-solver attitude with a little human touch, of course.

SO CLOSE, YET SO FAR!

Courtesy: dinospike.com

It is 10.30 p.m. Two teammates are in office working late to finish up some work. The people in question are inexperienced fresh graduates who have joined the organisation few months back. They are putting in their best possible efforts to learn and get up to speed with other experienced team members.

Teammate 1: This is damn complicated. I was trying to figure this thing out, but to no avail. Thanks to XYZ (senior member), who just explained to me all about this. Now I understand it but right now do not have the strength to work on it right away. Let's go home, cook some food, and then burn some midnight oil.

Teammate 2: I think that is fair. It's not that we were passing time. We can work in our beds from home a little relaxed.

Next morning.

Teammate 2: Hey, I heard you got called in the cabin. Everything okay?

Teammate 1: Actually, everything okay with me. But, I am not sure about him in the cabin. (Smirks)

Teammate 2: What did he say?

Teammate 1: I don't know. But, he is sitting on a burner I think. He needs therapy man! He asked that why did we leave early. I mean, can you imagine? What clock he has? Then he just blasts about how the performance is not good and it was not late as he was also up. He is a moron or what? I thought he had a wife and kids at home. If he is not happy at home and stays here, how that is anybody else's fault. Sadistic he is. Doesn't live and doesn't let live. I was so excited to work on this thing and learning it, but now don't feel like it. On top of that when I start explaining, he shuts me down saying that he doesn't want excuses. Well, someone tell Mr Sadistic who doesn't like being at home that reasons are not excuses. I stayed till late. When we went back, our cooking gas ran out. We didn't even have anything to eat. Somehow we managed something and then it was too late. You tell me, what is even humanly possible to do anything after that? I think his wife is a husband-beater (chuckles). That is why he doesn't go home himself and lets out the frustration on everybody. Also, is there a rule that juniors have to compulsorily spend fourteen hours in office? They say that put in your best efforts and rest will happen. We are doing that, aren't we? But if we take some time to learn something, then we will take that much time. His cribbing and blasting won't help. Moreover, he doesn't even want to get to the root of the problem. He could have had a healthy discussion and figured out the root cause, and it would have been best for everyone. He has to put even a little bit of effort to understand people in his team, which he won't. If this is the thing, then why do they put "has to be a people person" in the job description of managers. If he doesn't have a personal life, that doesn't mean we don't too

Teammate 2: Whoa, whoa! You are all filled up. The meeting would have been interesting then. (winks)

Teammate 1: (smiles) Dude, I think we should contribute and gift him a nice holiday just for himself, away from his wife. He needs to get off the stove.

In the meantime, the manager was thinking 'I need to tighten up these freshers. I will make it a mandate just for them that they have to give sixteen hours of work every day for next week at least.'

And trust me, IT guys in India will relate to this. This is not an exaggeration, but managers can unfortunately do this many times.

I faced something similar myself at the start of my career. Once my manager called me and told that I was not showing enough seriousness and was leaving early. I didn't even have dedicated project work that time. I was perplexed. When this happened the third time, I replied that *I don't leave early. I leave on time. I come in at 8.30 a.m. and leave at 6 p.m. How is that early? He only wants me in the chair, even if all I do is use the Internet and chat with my girlfriend. I think I would rather than go home and chat. If there is work that is urgent, I would stay myself. Further, if ever there is a lapse in my work, then sure you can question me. Even if you say that I should stay and study and improve my knowledge, well, that also I would like to do from home once the office time is up as I have computer and Internet at home.*

It is amazing how definition of office time changes for managers in India.

Keeping these things aside, the point in contention is that subordinates feel that managers are supposed to look for root causes of the problems and not symptoms and solve them. And that is exactly what they don't do is what subordinates feel.

People work to live and not live to work. I agree that sometimes work is such that you have to spend extra hours and people don't crib about it unless that becomes a routine. And even then if there is one slip by someone, he gets blasted, and manager just focuses on what he wants to see and conveys that rather than finding out why the slip happened in the first place. It comes across then that the manager or the company simply doesn't care about the employee but only about the work. Many a time, people are not in the highest of spirits because they have a life outside of office and could be facing some personal problems. Sometimes few misses happen because of it. Or there could be some intangible problem which is affecting the performance. So getting down to the root of it is most important to prevent it from repeating.

Created using dinospike.com

Early in my career, one of my friends was receiving regular feedbacks that she needed to improve her performance. After few repetitive lapses, her manager called her. She was mighty scared to go in, but when she came out, she had some kind of resolve about her to improve herself. What was different about this conversation?

Friend's manager: Hi. Please have a seat.
She sits down.
Manager: How are you doing?
Friend: I am doing okay. Trying my best.
Manager: I have some feedback for you. But before that, I would like to know what your take is. Are you facing some problems, are there any other issues you would want to talk about? I can give you all sorts of feedback, but I won't even know whether they are valid or not. I think you have the potential but then somehow it is not translating into output. What do you think?

My friend told me later that after this, she really felt comfortable and at ease so much so that she was ready to openly discuss about her shortcomings with the hope that the manager who was the leader for her would help her fix issues rather than just put it on her with extra pressure.

Friend: Initially, I would admit that I probably did not take it seriously. I heard from everywhere that other internal projects were just going on and on and so ours being an internal project too, I thought deadlines are not that rigid and we could take our time to learn as the project was meant for us to learn.

Manager: Well, I would say it is exactly the opposite. Internal projects are for your learning too, but they are rolled off to solve some organisational needs internally as well. And since these projects are totally owned by us, the deadlines are even more rigid and monitored. I agree there are few projects which are way off target as per the initial estimates, but there are many factors in that and it is not a general case for internal projects. Good that you mentioned this so that I could clear this, because my success also depends on your success. If the team doesn't do well, I also have to take a lot of hit from seniors. For the other point, yes, these projects are also meant for your learning but that does not mean you will have an open-ended time. You would be given certain relaxations which are not possible on client projects, but deadlines are sacrosanct.

Friend: Yeah, I understand that now. There is one more thing. I am a little slow in grasping and implementing these things. I am trying my best. There are few others of my batch who are good at it and better than me, so when someone compares us, I will always appear as underperformer.

Manager: Listen, we selected all of you for our company. There was no way we could have selected you or anybody else if you were not good. May be others have had some prior exposure, but we see that you have the same potential. It is a matter of generating interest. Initially, you will have to force yourself to put in extra efforts and then you will see that once you start understanding, you will develop interest and then everything will fall in place. Always remember, no one is better than you unless you allow them to be. So I know that you have great potential and it is only a matter of time and effort that you unravel it. If you are reluctant to talk to me all the time, talk to your seniors. They will chalk out a plan. Follow it and take feedback. You are as good as anyone, so don't think otherwise. Pull up your socks and start your engine.

Friend: Thanks a lot for the suggestions. I will get down to it straightaway and regularly share with you the progress.

Manager: That's great. And if you want to talk about any issue, you can reach out to me anytime.

When my friend came out, she was all praises for her manager, and what a leader and guide he was! And that was something very unusual I was hearing from anyone about their manager. If only a majority of managers understood these finer points, the term manager would be so much looked upon with respect rather than scorn. The incident got etched into my memory, and when I became the manager, whenever I tried to address the root cause, the people responded and demonstrated drastic changes. Even my friend started putting in extra effort with determination, and sometime later, she even got a pat for understanding a complex piece and delivering the work with minimal guidance. That boosted her morale further, and over time, she was one of the good performers. Managers have to be leaders. They have the power to make or break people. Why not focussing on making them?

<u>Moral:</u> Feedback discussions are a golden opportunity to unearth and address the root cause of the problem. Managers are so close to doing it by calling in such a meeting, yet so far by not utilising it in a proper way.

TO LEAD OR TO MANAGE, THAT IS THE QUESTION

Losing:

Created using dinospike.com

That is the question indeed. And one hell of a question. To find the answer, just ask a subordinate. People hate to work for managers, but they love to work with leaders. Please notice what I had said above, it is work 'for' managers, but love to work 'with' the leaders. That is the first difference between being a manager and a leader. In my experience, this topic has always been dicey and in most cases, not even thought about. That is why, here, I can't put many anecdotes or satirical situations. These are insightful few pages in this book. Getting back to the first difference. Even by mere listening to the phrase 'work for' doesn't inspire much. No one wants to work for anyone. People want to work for themselves. But managers always make people work for them and also give out that impression. That is precisely why people hate working for them. Leaders, on the other hand, are connected to people. They always exude a vibe of working 'with' everyone rather than 'for'. Consequently, people work 'for' themselves 'with' the leader.

In a set-up like a manufacturing plant, where manager has to get work done by wage workers, it is imperative that you are a pure manager. But, for knowledge-based industries, where qualifications, aspirations, pride, motivation, and respect are involved, nothing much can be achieved by being a mere manager. Managers ought to be leaders. Leadership qualities are mostly innate and inherent in few people, but with careful observation and effort, it can be developed. Managers understand hard rules and processes, while leaders understand these as well as people they work with. Managers inspire fear of authority. Leaders inspire faith and action. With leaders, people work for themselves, and that is why they have extra zeal for it, which ultimately benefits the organisation too. With managers, people work for managers, which is bound to cut that zeal down considerably.

Then why do managers remain managers and not become leaders. Being a manager is a mighty tough job too, but being a leader is even tougher. Also, managers get so involved with managing that they do not pay attention to the other aspects and thus do not develop into leaders.

What do we know Bill Gates or Steve Jobs as? Managers? Or leaders? That is the difference I am trying to point out. Both of them were very much in management positions, but they were leaders by role and that is why we know them and not the countless 'managers' in both these organisations.

Leaders address the beliefs and values of other people. They ignite people from within, and that is why people follow them. Also, they follow for their own sake, because it is their inner self that has been awoken and so they do it for themselves. Leaders understand people and act accordingly.

Leaders are very good at knowing themselves too. They don't live in a delusion about their abilities, values, or emotions. They also know their limitations and accept them without feeling sorry for it. They just accept it openly. When people see that, they relate to him. They see that he is also human and that is why trust him more and follow him more because despite his few limitations, he is really a capable person and is able to touch others with this thoughts and actions. Managers, on the other hand, in most cases, give an impression of being the supreme power and authority. Sometimes, they behave and talk as if they themselves had never done anything wrong in life. And that is what people do not relate to. They sense hypocrisy there. Why then anyone love to work for them? They will just complete their formalities of work and leave.

Leaders also have great control over their emotions, words, and actions. They know how to calmly handle things in the best possible way. They don't let off the steam easily. And if you ask subordinates, managers are mostly on the boil. Managers scream, scold, and put the onus and pressure of performance on the others. Leaders respect their teammates, own the problems, and work with the team to resolve it. They know that in tough times, if you are there for your people, rather than boiling over, the team will work extra hard to correct the mistakes and will respect and trust the leader. When people commit mistakes and realise it, they will feel very let down for themselves. In that scenario, no one wants someone else to be hanging a sword over them or breathing down their neck. It is in these times that people see that leaders stand with them, but managers stand on the opposite side. That is why leaders are followed and respected, while managers are scorned at.

One of the other most important traits of a leader is that they understand and empathise with their people. They are emotionally aware, considerate, and receptive too. On the other hand, I have seen managers who think that emotions are waste of time in getting work done. Almost all have 'I don't care' attitude. People then get a feeling that they are not even treated like living beings but just like physical assets for the company. Leaders seek out emotional cues from their people and are ever ready to lend an ear. Managers, though, in some rare cases are open to listening, but they wait for others to initiate and do not seek to find out or take the initiative of finding out whether something is wrong with his people. Therefore, leaders attract people, while managers repel.

Managers, direct. Leaders, guide. Leaders take onus on themselves and stand by the team. Managers first try to shield themselves. Leaders are patient, tolerant, and seek to address the root issue. Managers address only the symptoms and are much less tolerant.

Teammate 1: Hey, turn around just for a second.

Teammate 2: What happened? What is it?

Teammate 1: No, I was trying to find out where your circuitry and all are, because, that dude in the cabin surely thinks that we are all robots here.

Teammate 2: That ways, he has a very fertile mind. He doesn't see people. He sees work machines.

Teammate 1: That is why these people are supposed to be the leaders in the company. A leader always sees others as fellow human beings rather than process compliant, programmed bots.

Winning:

Created using dinospike.com

<u>Moral:</u> People love to work with leaders and do not work for managers. Young managers, don't be managers; strive to be leaders.

BEINGS,
NOT MATERIALS

Created using dinospike.com

The most commonly used term for people in IT industry is 'resources'. Sure they are knowledge resources, but that is now how you address people. People do not connect with that. It sounds purely material and gives the feeling that people are perceived, just as mere things, to achieve company's objective.

The job description of most managers specify being able to manage people. 'People Management,' as it is called, is on the job description of every manager. However, I feel that people management is the biggest oxymoron when it comes to knowledge-based industries. People are people. People are not time, money, materials, or schedule that they have to be 'managed'. In such an industry, people cannot be managed. People can be either led, inspired, motivated, or mentored. When you manage people, what happens is exactly what is happening now in the industry, people hating to work for managers. People need and want to be respected, not materialised. That is why people cannot be managed. There has to be a human touch. For human touch, the first requirement is to treat and address people as human. Most of those working in IT industries chose to be there. They are passionate about what they do. It is only fair when they expect they be treated in a certain manner. They expect, first and foremost, to be respected. We in IT, unfortunately, have become so used to calling people as resources that we sometimes don't even realise that we are talking about people. But somehow subconsciously everyone feels gutted by it, even though they have become used to it.

Teammate 1: Hey, java resource? How you doing? I heard they need a java guy. Sorry, java resource, in one project.

Teammate 2: What are you up to?

Teammate 1: I mean that is what we are, right? We are just resources, aren't we? So much so that even for direct introductions, this term is used, forget about talking when talking in third person. My manager today introduced me to the client as .NET 'resource'. He could have also used something else. Even .NET 'guy' would have been fine. What am I? Something the company has bought to use?

Teammate 2: Ha ha . . . true. Amazing thing is when it comes to management, they are management team or a project manager. Why don't they use management resource for themselves? Anyways, that is why after working all these years in a similar set-up, I have actually become like a resource. I do only what is told clear to me. No using extra brains. When I am treated like a programmed material, I should bloody behave like that as well.

That is why people management is a farce. In such industries, there is no need for a 'People Manager'. There is a need for 'People Leader'. If it was a line manager in a manufacturing set-up or unions, for example, 'People Manager' makes sense. But does IT operate like that? Then why the same management concepts are followed? It is like teaching kids of this tech age in a gurukul set-up. Of all the industries, IT is the newer, technologically advanced, and innovative industry. Then why borrow the management approaches from the older ones? Okay, when the industry started, few people adopted it and it worked in those times. But why do we have to keep practicing it in the same manner?

Manager: You have to take care of these things and think of alternatives. You are an experienced resource for the project. Use your brain a little bit.

Team lead: Well, I am not just a resource. I am not a utility or an infrastructure item. I am an expert in my field. And I did give alternatives and that is why the situation is not as bad as could have been. And if I am a resource, then you should not expect any brains out of me. Resources do not have brains.

Team lead leaves.

Manager (thinking): What happened to him? He got offended.

One of my friends recounted something similar to me once when he had gotten absolutely irritated by the bullying manager along with the resource thing which he hated. The problem here, like in many other cases, is that the management itself doesn't realise this, but it ticks the subconscious of majority of people who are referred to as resources.

Teammate 1: Oh no! The learnt guy has woken up again.

Teammate 2: What's up, dude?

Teammate 1: Nothing. The usual. Suddenly the learnt guy wakes up and asks details about training and self-learning I have undertaken while I wait to be assigned to the projects. He needs an update. It is so frustrating. He should be called the 'pestering manager' rather than the people or home manager as they term it. Nobody even knows this guy properly. He is just concerned about updates and plans about learning and nothing else at all.

Teammate 2: Just go and blabber something. In any case, he does not know anything. He just has to put it down somewhere and send it to higher-ups.

Teammate 1: Hell, yeah. That is what I do every time. It is only that it is irritating.

Some companies have a dedicated manager who 'manages' all the people who are on 'bench'. This can be anyone like 'home manager' or 'people manager'. The purpose, in organisational documents, of this person is very decorative. They are the people managers who look after the training needs, professional growth, and any issue resolution for the people who are not active on any client projects. But in reality, these managers only push training programmes and ask for updates from them. There is nothing like 'home' or 'people' about this manager.

If there is such a person, he has to connect with the people. He has to figure out ways of connecting with those people and be there to guide them and hear out their issues. He, of all people, cannot stick to just the processes and touch base with people only on predefined times and in predefined ways, just to complete that action item on his checklist.

Created using dinospike.com

I have personally seen people behave like that depicted in the above picture. And this is what will happen when you try to manage people.

<u>Moral:</u> Young managers, don't be just managers. Connect with people, personally. And remember, people are not just resources.

SHIT WILL HAPPEN.
BE AWARE

Created using dinospike.com

There is one thing which is omnipresent in all organisations no matter what the management says and claims. In some, it is to a lesser extent; in others, it is more pronounced. And that is politics. In companies, people may accept it or not, either politics is god or the means to reach god. Again, not everyone is involved in it. Some are damn good at it, and some just avoid it. It is easier to avoid politics by someone who are in the lower end of the ladder. As you go up, it is more difficult to avoid and, at the same time, has more impact on you if it hits you. However, there is a common ground. For anyone with even little bit of values, politics is shit, be it in the country or in the organisation. But staying out of it is not easy. To avoid politics, one has to be more aware and careful than when you indulge in it. I am no judge of anything. So if you are good at it, it is good for you that you use it because in my experience, people who are great at it tend to benefit a lot. After all, it is a pig fight. If you have to catch or fight a pig, you have to dive down into the mud. On the other hand, if you want to stay clear off the ditch, you need to be more aware and careful because when pigs fight, they splash too. If you are not careful for one moment, you never know what pile of mud flies across and hits you. And trust me, this mud is flying around all the time. And you do not want it to smack across your face and catch you unawares.

Created using dinospike.com

There are many reasons for this. There are some people who themselves do not believe that just with capability they can be visible or they can progress in the company. There are some for whom this is second nature, and they don't even know they are doing it. Some others do it because they get caught up in it and are forced to do it. But whatever it may be, no organisation is rid of it. Keep an open eye at all times. If you observe closely, with some practice, you will be able to make out at least three kinds of people practicing one form of politics or the other. The first kind of people is those who are bent over all the time for their superiors. You won't physically see it, but on close observation, you will be able to make out what I mean. Second kind is those who have at least three feet long tongues and have the ability to lick anything clean, if you know what I mean. The third kind is those who are combined form of the first and second kinds mentioned above and thus much more potent. In addition to this, these are extremely cunning and intelligent in this particular field, no matter how moronic or retarded they might be in the area in which they are actually supposed to be good. For these people, only they themselves exist and are not even bothered about anything else. Outside they will walk with pride because no one knows a thing that is actually happening inside the organisation. So that works out well for them.

Teammate 1: How come this guy gets promoted every cycle? Nobody likes the way he operates, and I don't see any worthwhile work he does.

Teammate 2: Obviously, you do not see this three feet tongue which is taken out in discussions which are beyond our level.

Teammate 1: Ya. That ways he has amazing talent. If there was a world cup for this, he would win hands down.

Teammate 2: Plus, have you heard the joke where people are stuck on a tree at different levels? That represents an organisation. People below can only see the person above from beneath. And no points for guessing what they see. Then it gets better. And since people above are above and stay there, only one thing ever comes down from them. Hope you get what I am conveying.

Teammate 1: Ha ha ha . . . I got it. That was an amazing one and an apt one I would have to say.

The situation is precarious even more for those who have just entered the lower levels of management. The stakes are high, and they do not have enough authority to control or impact these things.

Teammate 1: Why did you not get sent to onshore? You are more capable, and everyone would vouch for that, not just me.

Teammate 2: Well, how on earth am I supposed to know? I guess that guy has some special which I don't have, or rather, don't want to have.

If you have to or decide to take on the pig fight by not diving down in the mud, I suggest you have a ten feet rod to attack from way outside the mud pool. Otherwise, as they say, pigs will drag you down to their level and beat you with experience.

Politics can range from smallest of things to biggest of things in an organisation. I have seen managers just worry about their KPIs and not in the least caring anything about other people. They don't care if lives are being made or broken. They get up singing KPIs and go to sleep singing KPIs.

Teammate 1: This guy is always on about how his KPIs will be hit. It doesn't matter what is happening to people.

Teammate 2: I wonder if ever, although that is very difficult to imagine, he has even a romantic moment with his wife, I bet he is still thinking about KPIs.

To unfairly save themselves, they will always be ready to botch someone else up. The moot point is anyone going in new at the mid-lower level of management has to be extra careful and also keep in mind that he doesn't turn out the same when he progresses. Although, there might be outward success by indulging in it, there won't be much respect. And I think, respect is important. Everyone has to make a choice of their own.

<u>Moral:</u> Be aware, be careful, and stay true to your values because shit happens.

**IDEALISM IS A MYTH.
IT EXISTS ONLY IN
DICTIONARY**

Created using dinospike.com

Of all the reasons, one of the most predominant reasons for war and all the dirt around in the world or an organisation is pure, inconsiderate, callous, and lustful ambition. Look around, and in almost all the things, you will see it. It is when people are blinded by their own ambitions that they do not even bother to look around and see whom are they trampling along to get what they want. Don't get me wrong. I am not saying being ambitious is negative. Having an ambition is one of the most important things in life. As the famous roman emperor Marcus Aurelius said, *A man's worth is no greater than the worth of his ambitions*, is absolutely true. What I am talking about is the extreme situation of it. Although it is extreme, you will find and encounter it more frequently than you encounter other extreme occurrences. And if you get entangled in these plans, especially when they are of your superior, you stand to get hit in most novel and drastic ways.

It was only because of these kinds of ambition that even history teaches us that led to killing of kings or killing of one's own family to be the king. It has been at the root of all wars. And that kind of ambition is wrong.

Teammate 1: I am not getting any worthwhile work. Then at the end of the year, in appraisals, I would be told that I didn't do anything great so it is an average rating. I mean, to give me work is their responsibility. How that becomes my fault? And if I do something on my own accord, they will brush it and say that nobody told you to do that.

Teammate 2: I will tell you the secret story behind it. It is not even difficult to see if you think about it. See, you have shown that you have potential. So, if you are given good work all the time, you will prove good again and again. What happens then? Soon, you are knocking at the heels of superiors. They have to give you a good raise and an elevation in position to satisfy you. And how can they do it when your superior is still there in his chair? He has to go up to allow you in that place. Till he goes up, he cannot let you come up close enough to him. And he cannot move that fast up, because deep down, he knows he is not that good. So he has to stall cases like you. Only way is not give you a chance to prove, or something which you like and would excel at. Nobody then is going to question anybody.

I will agree that the above scenario doesn't happen everywhere, but this was one of the most surprising thoughts I ever heard from a colleague.

Excess of anything is bad. Ambition is no different. I saw one other interesting thing in my career. Before going into it, I would like to advise managers, especially the young managers, to be extra careful in cases when someone has recently been promoted to a larger role and you are to report to him. If that person doesn't have his head on his shoulders, the situation would go spiralling down before you know it. One of my friends joined the company as a project manager. Up till that point, he had a colleague who was the senior manager. Everything was fine till that point. The senior manager was appreciative of his work and guided him well. Then the senior manager got promoted, and my friend was to report to him. After few weeks, there was visible change in the attitude of the senior manager (now the director). He started reeking off power. His demeanour changed to one which exuded that 'I am the boss here and I have the power.' 'I bet, sometimes, he also fantasised himself as the He-Man,' remarked my friend. Now, to prove to his superiors that he was doing something worthwhile, he started to micromanage; once in a while, he randomly started sending feedbacks to the senior folks which according to my friend were not always valid feedbacks. The responses of my friend reached only till the director, but director's initial mail was always bcc-ed to the senior management. Director started becoming more and more aggressive at everything. He started behaving as if he controlled the office, and more so, even showed it. My friend wondered what he had got caught up in. He somehow rode the tide, but it was very difficult.

This was a classic case of feeding your ambitions on someone else's cost. The director was hell-bent on proving his utility and excellent performance since he took the new role that he did not even regard what he was unfairly doing to others. This happens more with people who themselves can't believe that they reached a certain position. They cannot come to terms with it. They are more insecure and jittery. To hide all this, they resort to these things to build a false tough exterior for no reason so that they are not questioned enough. In addition, in most cases, they have not held a position of responsibility in their entire life, so when it comes to them, they go berserk thinking that while it lasts, let them make use of it.

Again, this is not true for everyone. However, if you observe people carefully, you will be able to make this out. If you talk about idealism, this is far from it. But that is the truth. Nothing is ideal, and the only solution is to be aware and observant all the time.

Lot of times, in the case of growing companies, positions are created in view of the expansion. When that happens, some people get to elevated roles by the virtue of just being in the right place at the right time. That is counterproductive in many ways. The idea of top management is very much right. When the company is on the growth path, they have to be scalable, and so some restructuring has to happen to allow the company to be prepared for times ahead. But no matter how much good the intention of the top brass is, if that thinking doesn't percolate down to mid-management, it creates more dissatisfaction than action. For example, in one of the small companies my friend was working, the position of director was introduced. But there was no chalked out plan as to what the director would actually and specifically do. The result was even being the director, he was still involved with project management. What made it worse was, he became more involved so much so that many times he used to subvert the manager who was actually managing the team and direct the team himself. He became over-aggressive and over-intrusive with absolutely no regard for others. His sole motive, it seemed, was to keep impressing the senior management that he still had lot of work and was closely involved. In situations like these, the less appropriate people tend to become even more ambitious totally in the wrong way.

Organisations should also think about the repercussions of appointing people while expanding the company. It would be better to either wait for the right person to be able to take that role or clearly communicate the role and expectation as per the philosophy of the organisation. I have personally seen the culture of an organisation seriously dented by things like this. In this particular case, the director had no business in day-to-day activities of the project. The manager was reporting to him, and he could have got the requisite information from the manager rather than meddling himself.

If we look back at history books, we can note that wars have been fought because of either women or lustful ambition or because someone was a pure psychopath. In organisations, you will find that the source of all the dirt is either because of politics or callous ambitions. Even politics to some extent is because of uncontrolled ambitions. As I have already mentioned in the previous chapters, those involved in politics are the people with insecurity and three feet tongue with backs bent. And when all these are combined, it is as potent a combination as you will ever find.

Young managers should not only be aware of these things, but also make extra effort to keep themselves safe because the moment it gets out of hand, you will be the first scalp of that storm.

I have seen very senior people make comments that are uncalled for. This behaviour showed a glimpse of their personality and mentality.

Manager: I scolded that guy little while back. Now, when I went to the person next to him, he looked at me with a grimace. Think what you what, man, I am beyond you. You can't reach me.

Subordinate: Hmm . . . I saw he looked upset.

Manager: How do I care?

If a person is very confident of his position and authority, his statements won't reek of power hunger. I am still not sure what he meant by *I am beyond you.* These people think themselves to be the kings. I would like to say this as the 'I am HE-MAN' syndrome. Truth is he is farthest away from it than anyone else.

Once, the same person scolded a fresh graduate in the company as he thought that she was getting too much attention on the floor. I was appalled on hearing this. His job was just to see that the work gets done. Whether she is getting attention or not is not his concern. And practically, who, if not a girl, would get attention? Certainly not the oldie managers. Is he running a Taliban outfit or in a management role in a multinational organisation? It again brings out the point why would subordinates cringe if managers behave like this?

Thus, the younger generation has the extra responsibility of doing not only the right things but also in the right way.

<u>Moral:</u> If you want to find idealism, look in the dictionary. At present, you won't find it anywhere else, until you work to bring a semblance of it yourself.

YOU GOT A MIND AND MOUTH.
WELL . . . USE IT

Created using stripgenerator.com

Humans are the most intelligent species with a very well-developed brain. Thinking and analysing is a competency that makes humans so much more sustainable on the earth, as compared to other species. Humans are good at thinking, and thinking is the first step in achieving something. Sometimes, the thinking process is an end in itself. But, just good thinking and doing the job quietly won't get you anywhere in an organisational setup. Speaking is one of the most important thing in an organisation. In many cases, it is even more important than doing your work. I am talking in general here. If you are an average performer, but you speak and project your work, you could be counted among the best performers. Most people in management would disagree and say that work is all that matters and bosses only see who does work and who does not. I would admit, when I became the manager, I felt the same with people in my team who were not that outspoken. It is a little tough to have confidence on someone who doesn't speak much. Especially when someone is new in the organisation and his work has not been proven. But I remembered my initial days as a team member when I used to quietly do my work. No matter how well I did my work but still it was not seen. On becoming a manager, I made it a point to pay extra attention and observe those people more. I was myself surprised that one of the best performers in the team were the ones who spoke less.

In today's world, speaking out goes a long way. More so, if you are a manager. As a young manager, even if you are an introvert, think of it as part of your job and speak out. Speak to your team members, and speak out in front of your senior management. That gives you more visibility, and more than anything else, it might even save you in critical situations.

Young Manager 1: I do not understand the strategy. I do not know why the company is so heavily dependent on one account. I hope they have analysed what would happen if that account goes.

Young Manager 2: I know. But they never talk or discuss these kind of things with us. It is only resourcing and project management stuff. How does it matter? Let them do what they are doing.

The problem with this approach is that you cannot be sure that even the senior is doing the right thing all the time. Nobody is perfect; they might also miss few things or worse, might be ignorant about something, so you need to raise it. If you have thought about it, then better speak about it. Do not accept or take anything lying down. If, by any chance, something goes wrong with some strategy, the management will start pruning the management layer from your level. Ultimately, you will lose out. And trust me, you will find lots of duffers in the top brass as well. Some are there just because they started something, or it may be the classic case of being at the right place at right time. And, they won't be the ones to go. They will make everyone else go in times when something goes wrong with the strategy.

We have been given a brain to think. That's all right. But, we have been given a mouth too. And the mouth doesn't have to serve the purpose to be rude or abusive but to speak up when it is right to put forward your opinions. Many times, young managers, down the level, just reserve themselves and do not speak up thinking that it might not go well with others. But think, these young managers became managers after having gone through some of the toughest competition in the country to get that education and be qualified. If they achieved that, there should be no reason to doubt themselves and be quiet. Who knows, they might be the smartest in the whole hierarchy. Even if nobody listens or pays heed to it, and if something which you actually talked about happens, you can at least say, *Well, you know what, I told you so.* That might also safeguard you against a calamity, and also, people would at least then listen to you going forward. So it is a win-win situation. However, you should be careful not to be authoritative. Do not speak in a way that others feel that you think of them to be fools. Be respectful, but be professionally assertive too. Give hard logic and reasoning without hurting anybody's ego. People, as they go up, have a tendency to develop really inflated egos. Never hurt that unless you know for 200 per cent sure that the battle you are starting is yours. If the senior management and the company culture is as candid as most of them claim, the job is little easier. Otherwise, this is one of the trickiest of situations to deal with. Some of the seniors are too desperate to make their impression to their superiors. They might play down your thoughts and propel their own to get more visibility. Ultimately, they might use their ultimate weapon of shutting you up by using their number of years of experience to make you feel you don't know enough. My advice is do not argue. Do not get into that duel. Calm down, and when you get a chance to speak to even higher management, be it at some lunch or office party, casually make the background and slip in your thoughts. If that works, great! Otherwise, you will have to keep patience. At least you tried and people heard at least something from you. You cannot try to be a maverick and do an 'Arnold Schwarzenegger' stuff in office to get everyone's ear. Keep your cool.

Created using stripgenerator.com

Moot point is don't try any stunts, but don't be mute as well. If you are not speaking, organisation will not even recognise your presence. And then, when someday, if you speak, it won't register in their heads that you had something to offer and they will just pass it over. I have myself experienced being ignored completely. I was not a speaker in the team. And when I did speak, it wasn't even acknowledged at times. Speaking is at the core of the job of a manager. Be it to the subordinates or to the people above, speaking is the mantra.

<u>Moral:</u> If you do not speak up, you are just a statue for the office. It makes other people's job less difficult to bypass you and get visible at your cost.

SPEAKING FRENCH TO A CHINESE WON'T WORK

Created using stripgenerator.com

The basic law of communication is to send a message in a form that the recipient can understand. This concept works at many levels, rather than just at the language and cultural level. People do not pay attention to this in great detail. Every individual is different. Everyone has a different frequency on which he understands things the most. That is why some people connect better with some and not so well with others. It is only when you communicate in a manner that the recipient is most receptive to, that, you would be able to get through to him. To be able to communicate in a right manner, you have to be a good observer of people. You have to be able to understand the other person quickly so that you can tune in on his frequency. This tuning to a particular frequency is what makes few professionals great. Some people just seem to get everyone on board with them, and some struggle to convince people even on most obvious things. This skill is mostly innate, but I have seen many people who have developed it over time. It takes lot of effort in terms of observation and practice. It also takes lot of effort in terms of controlling or masking your emotions. If you give in to emotions, you will not be able to tune to that perfect frequency. Continuing from the last chapter, speaking out is the core dish, but customising your communications as per each individual is the real garnishing on that dish, which not only makes it taste better, but also makes it even look 'delicious'. To assert this point that how important it is to communicate in a right manner, just look at all the famous leaders. All of them have had the great quality of communicating with people by matching their frequency. Even when they addressed the public, they would automatically and inherently sense the general frequency the public as a whole was. That is why they were able to connect and move the public by just words.

In organisations today, if you just speak up without any finesse, you might land into trouble more often than not. When you are making a point to someone, you have to gauge what channel is the most receptive one for the other person. If you do not tap that channel, the other person will, in most cases, take you in the exact opposite way than what you intended, and then, everything can turn hostile and irreparable.

Teammate 1: That guy is a crazy man. He is sitting on a grenade. He might blow off real soon.
Teammate 2: Ha ha ha . . . What happened?

Teammate 1: Nothing. I just went up to him and said that the way we are doing it is not right and I have thought of a better way about the thing the VP was talking about today in the meeting. He didn't even listen to what I had to say.

Teammate 2: Obviously. He is not one of those who likes to hear that he is wrong. If he was sitting on a grenade after the VP talk, you went and ignited it. You were right, but you need to say it differently when you say it to him.

Teammate 1: What is that? I just said it plain and simple.

Teammate 2: Wait. Let me try. Since he did not hear you, I will try to tell the same idea. If it works, I will tell you what I said.

Teammate 2 goes in the manager's cabin and comes out smiling after few minutes.

Teammate 1: What happened? Seems like you got through. What did you say?

Teammate 2: I just said I wanted some of his guidance and expertise on something regarding what the VP said today. That, I was thinking of something which could be a possible alternative to the problem but it was best if he validated it and then put it forward as it would put more weight in it. He then heard me out and agreed. Then he said that he would say it and mention me. I then told him that you and I both were discussing and it was actually your thought. He took that also very well.

Teammate 1: I need to learn that.

Teammate 2: Of course, you do. People are not friends here that they will take your straight talk. Some people do. It is okay with them. With our manager specifically, remember, he can never hear that he is wrong, especially from a subordinate. You need to encode your statements accordingly in that case.

I am not talking about buttering people. I am talking about framing your thoughts better so that the other person would receive it better. It is best for you. People higher up many times develop big egos. You have to factor that in. You cannot afford to hurt it. You need to polish it sometimes to get your thoughts through. Then, you would also be visible to him and others that you offered solutions, because you were on his frequency and he saw merit in you and your opinions.

Managers, on the hand, need to be as objective as possible. Do not develop a big ego. Many great people in history fell because of their great egos. That is a straight path downhill. You might not like it sometimes, but unless someone is overtly rude, you need to hear it objectively without letting your ego or any other emotion come in between. That is when a manager stands to gain the most and also earn respect from others. That is when a manager will be most effective because the manager will not have all the solutions all the time and input from others might prove to be valuable. A manager, thus, has to be attuned to multiple frequencies. Everyone then will be appreciative that they do not have to do extra to be able to communicate with the manager.

Created using stripgenerator.com

While some of the team members might be attuned to your frequency, not all are. And then they would feel that every time they have a conversation with you, it is like banging their head on the wall in a soundproof room. Managers cannot be like that. That is why he needs to be attuned to all the frequencies, especially his team member's.

Young managers need to focus in both directions. Their teams, as well as their bosses, because most of the time, they would be in situations where they need to put their point across to their bosses. To do that, they need to customise their communication in a way that their boss is most receptive to it. And trust me, with little observation and effort, it can be developed, even if you do not have it naturally. I speak this from my observation and experience. I was pathetic at this even though I was good at observing. With time, however, I feel I have myself improved and to a large extent it works, as recently, I have been able to make more people listen more receptively to me. You cannot be aggressive in conveying to someone who is innately aggressive himself. He will attack back and not listen to any meritorious points you might have. To someone who is an egotist, you cannot even hint that he was wrong. He will cut you out straight away. Some people listen well in a formal setting, while some listen well in a causal talk over coffee. The point is you need to mould the conversation accordingly so that the other person is in the best possible state to listen and pay attention to you.

<u>Moral:</u> Customised communications is the key to be able to get through more people more easily.

FEAR OR NOT,
RIGHT IS RIGHT

Created using dinospike.com

As they say, last but not the least, I would like to talk about the mundane, widely talked, hardly followed, and rather taken for granted topic. That is about values: human, professional, and moral values. A person is remembered fondly, or with a scorn, based on what values he exhibits in his life. Money and professional success is a yardstick, which people think of much later when they remember a person. To be respected, to be considered a leader, you got to exhibit through your actions what values you have. If money and material things are more important to someone, rather than being a man of value, then you should not be the ones who curse our corrupt politicians for just making money and not caring about others. At a lower level, you would be doing the same. I know it is not easy to always be doing the right things. Many a times, there will be pressure from all sides to do something which you do not agree to. There will be people who will try to scare you in an attempt to force you to do something they want you to do. However, when your actions impact someone else, you need to stand up for the right. As they say, courage is not lack of fear, courage is standing up in spite of the fear. Fear is something which is a great deterrent for doing something. On the other hand, it is also something which, many times, compels people to do certain things.

I know, all this seems like a preaching and everybody knows this, but when it comes to real life, many people do not remember or practice any of it. If you look at your whole life from the beginning, you will see that job is just one of the many things you do. Therefore, even if it is the fear of something happening at the workplace, standing up is important. Everyone working in the IT industry is a qualified professional. You yourself change jobs frequently. Why give someone the power to make you feel scared about anything? Be fearless in face of anything. Keep six months' salary separately, and as a last resort, be prepared to walk away if something is absolutely unacceptable to you. That will make others be scared of you. That will enable you to do things right the right way, no matter what.

Many times, many people are made scapegoats for something they had no part in. Don't be a part of that dirt if you are in midst of something like that, be it for your juniors or for your seniors.

Values have become like milk and apples. Everyone knows it is good to have them every day, but very few of us actually take it. We lecture everyone possible on values but seem to ignore it all together when it comes to practicing them. We say the system is like that, we cannot do anything, and we have to do the way something is currently being done. Well, I would say, it is a matter of choice. And, there is always a choice. It is only up to us to choose it or ignore it.

Created using stripgenerator.com

Teammate 1: They are looking to screw someone up. The project has gone downhill. But the fact is that no single person is responsible. Everyone is responsible. The most, client is responsible. But to show some action and send some message, someone will be screwed. Sad part is everybody knows this but no one can do anything.

Teammate 2: Well, you know it. Speak up. Can you live with the baggage that you could have tried but didn't? I can't. What are you scared of? At max, you will get on the wrong foot of these guys, your hike won't be much citing your attitude, or at most, your job will go. Dude, for someone like you, there are plenty of jobs in the market. Do you want to work with these kind of people?

There are few things which are right no matter what. Do right, and be right. Values have become synonymous to hypocrisy in a way. Everyone talks about it, but no one knows how to practice it. Do not put it on the shelf. Young managers have the responsibility to do right and also to undo the wrong practices with resolve, grit, and guts.

Created using dinospike.com

<u>Moral:</u> Values are what make a person. They are not just decorative words. Do right, the right way. Fear or not, right is right.